ELLIOTT NEGIN

CELEBRITIES SWEEPSTEAKS

 Methuen

New York   London   Sydney   Toronto

To Trudy Rosen (my mommy)
and
to Larry Paros, friend and collaborateur.

Library of Congress Cataloging in Publication Data

Negin, Elliott, 1954-
  Celebrities sweepsteaks.

  1. Biography—20th century—Caricatures and
cartoons. 2. Fame—Caricatures and cartoons.
3. American wit and humor, Pictorial. I. Title.
NC1429.N43A4 1979 741.5'973 79-17133
ISBN 0-416-00161-0

FIRST EDITION

Published in the United States of America by Methuen, Inc.
733 Third Avenue, New York, N.Y. 10017

ISBN—0-416-00161-0

Printed in the United States of America

For those of you in our viewing audience playing *Celebrities Sweepsteaks* for the first time, here's how to play the game:

Beginning on the next page is a series of drawings which illustrate the names of famous people. You have exactly 60 seconds in which to name that celebrity. (You may take more time, just don't tell anybody.)

The answer (name) is printed upside down below each drawing.

tuesdayweld

captainkangaroo

farrahfawcett

wcfields

petergraves

jackarmstrong

shanana

elizabethtaylor

markspitz

soupysales

einstein

thecaptainandtennille

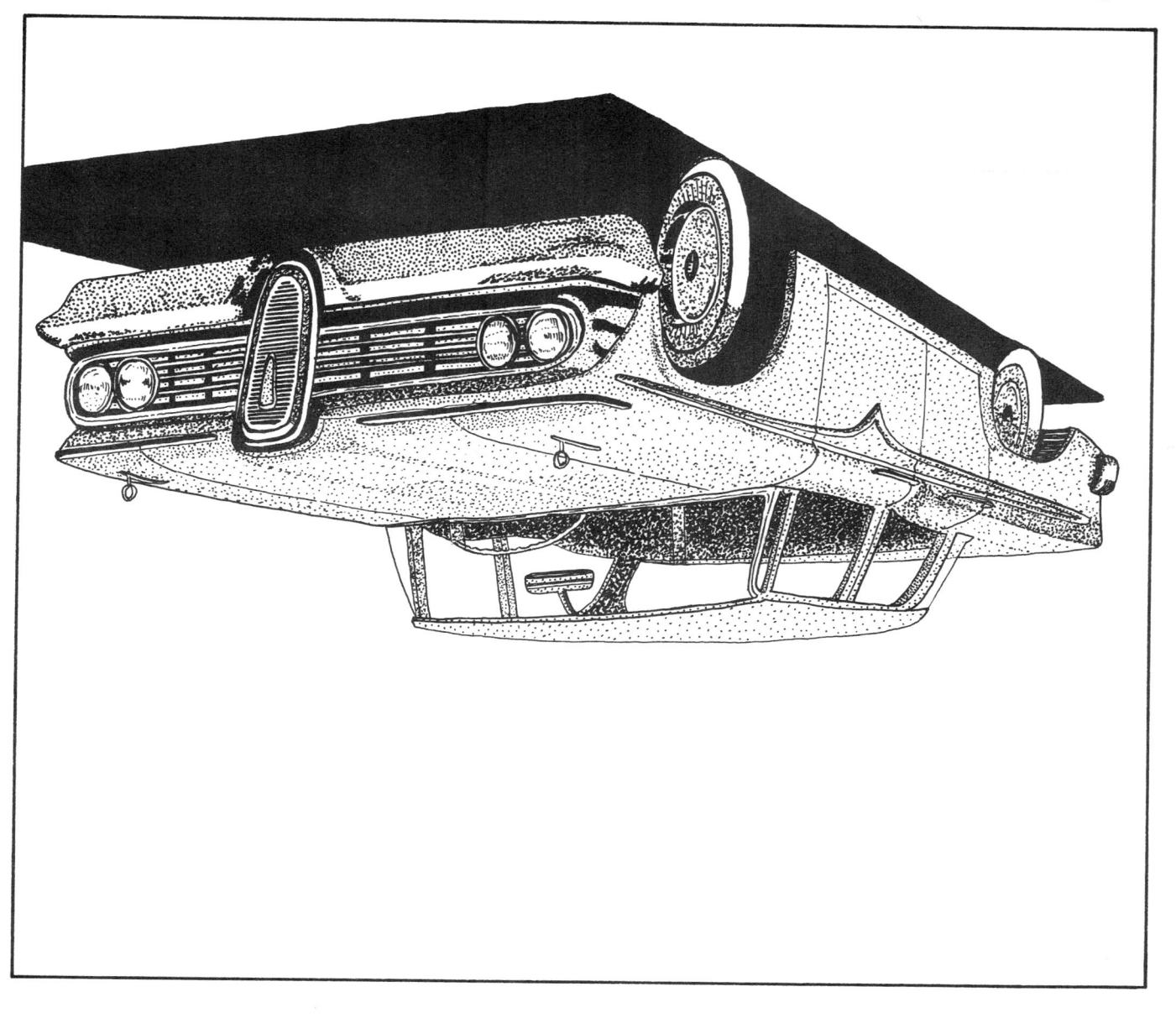

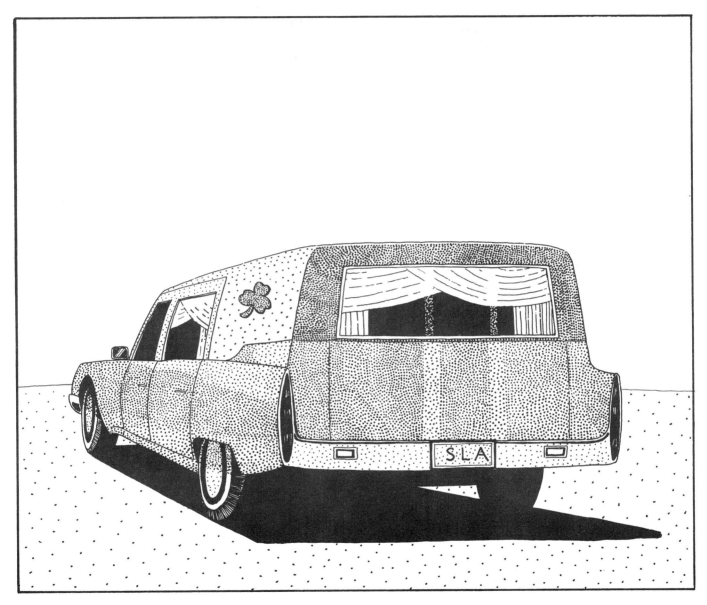

pattyhearst

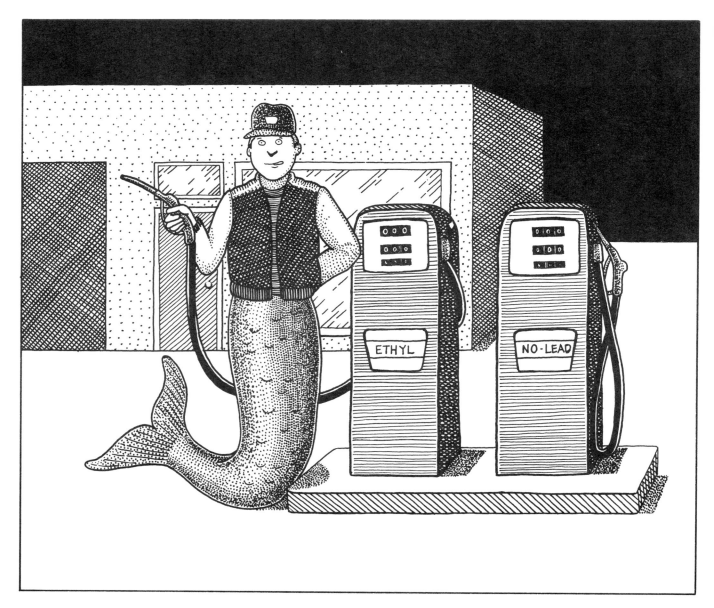

ethelmerman

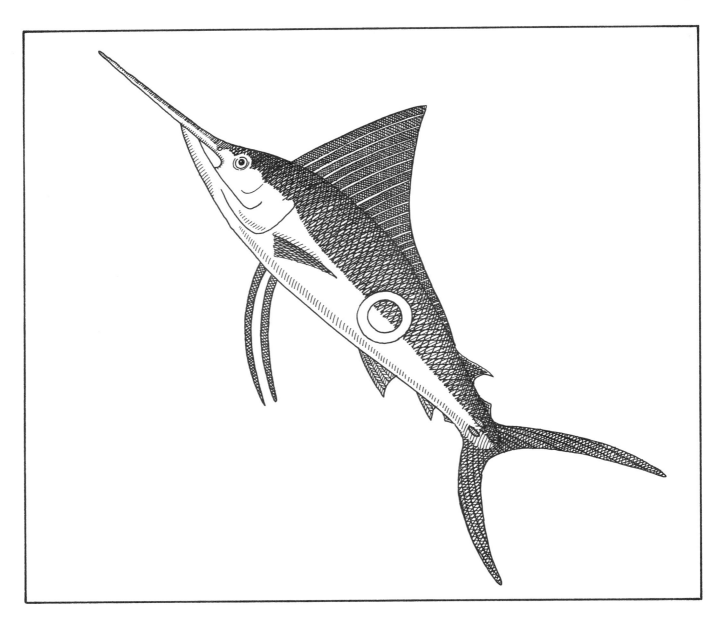

marlonbrando

buffalobill

popejohnpaul

eydiegorme

generalelectric

bishopsheen

totiefields

bertlance

slimpickens

noamchomsky

jacklemmon

catfishhunter

shelleywinters

montyhall

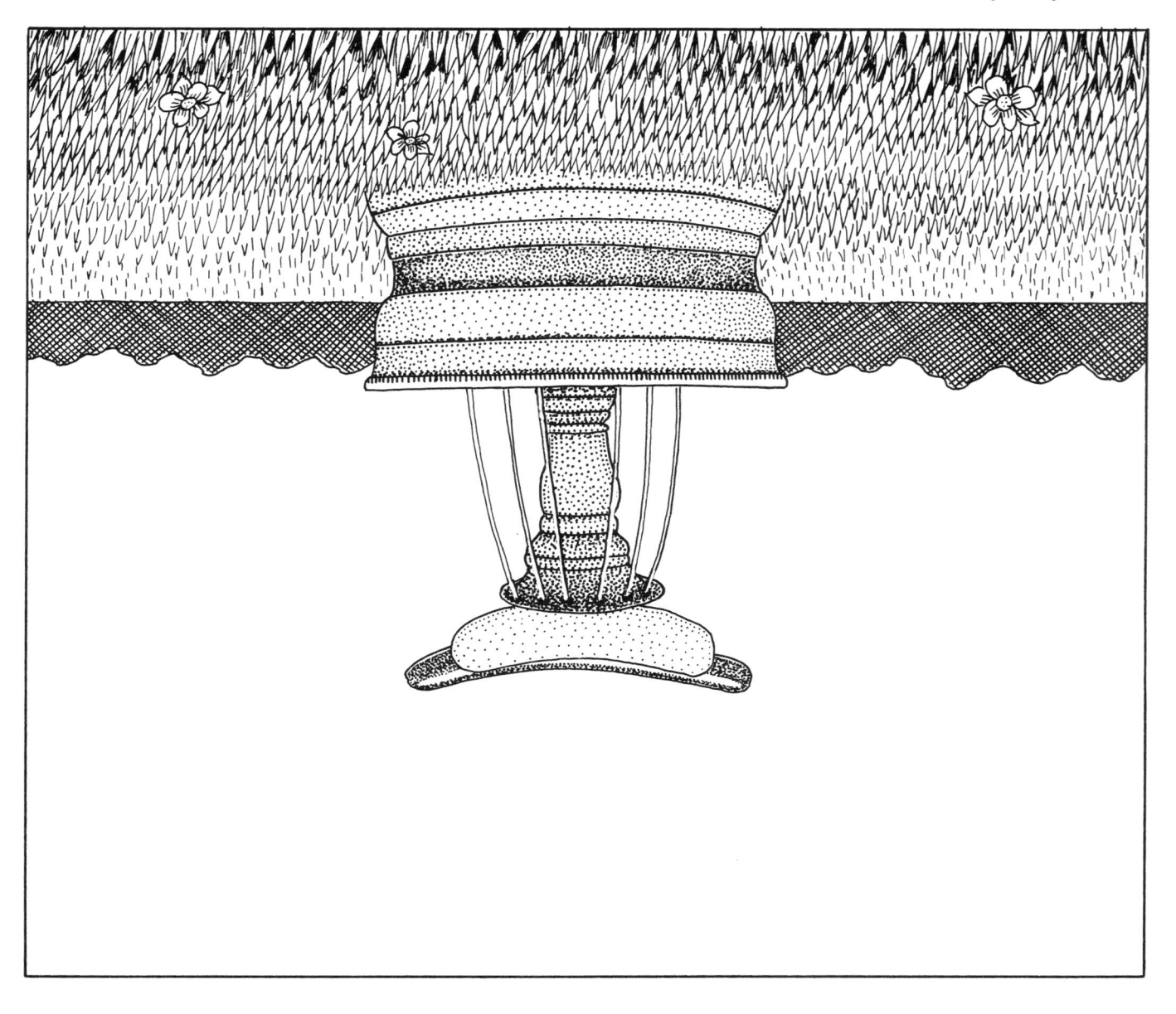

dinahshore

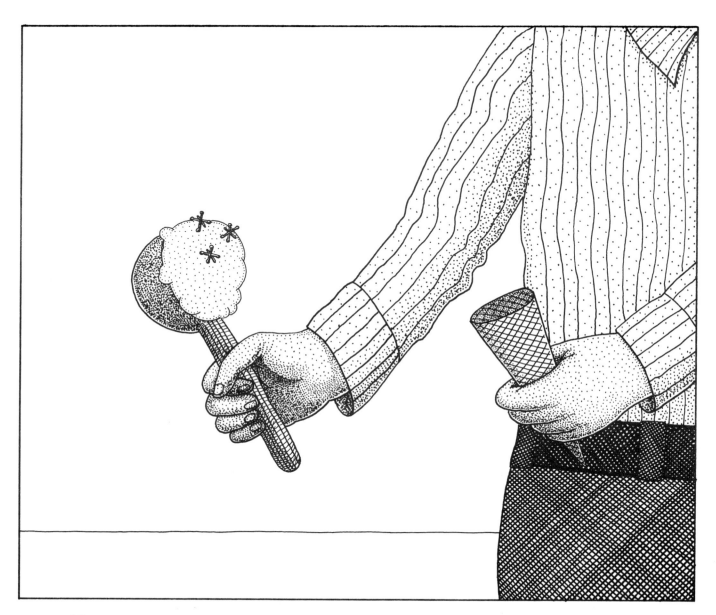

robinhood

frankenstein

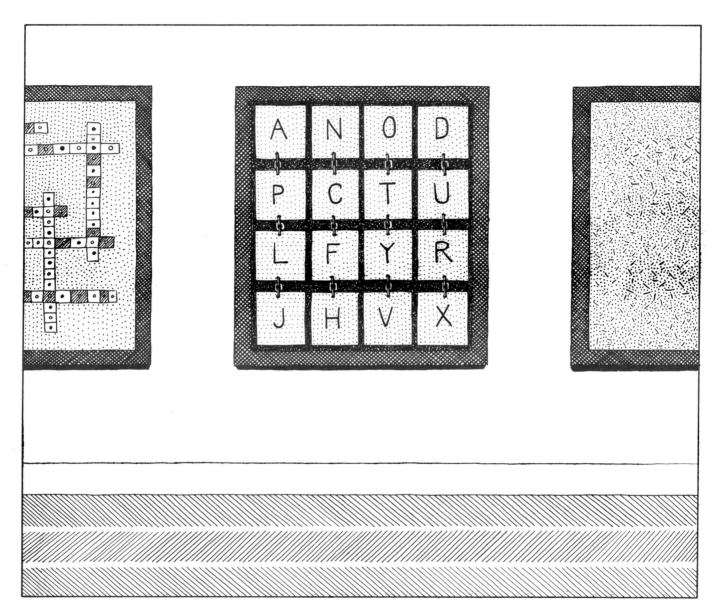

howdydoody

carriefisher

normanmailer

jimmabors

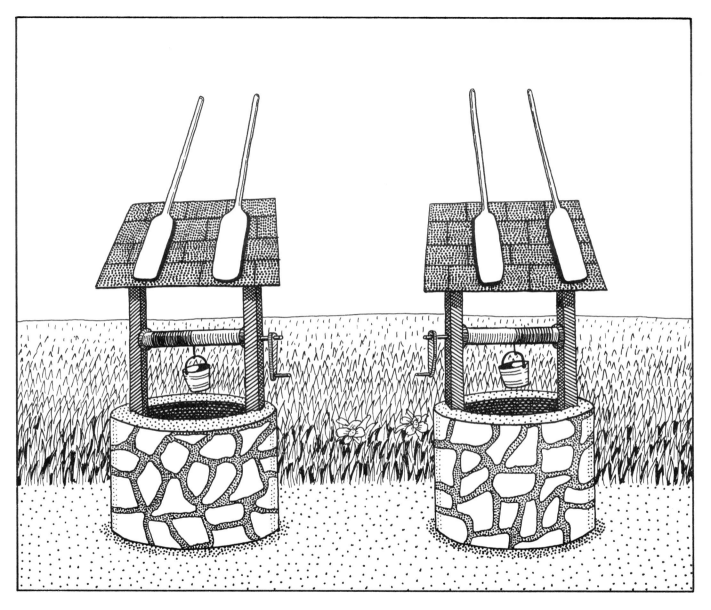

orsonwelles

colonelsanders

castroconvertible

thestlouiscardinals

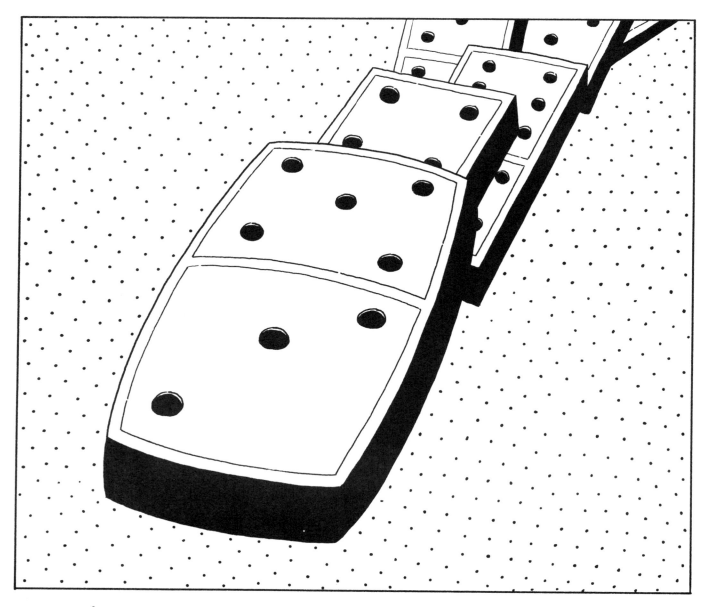

fatsdomino

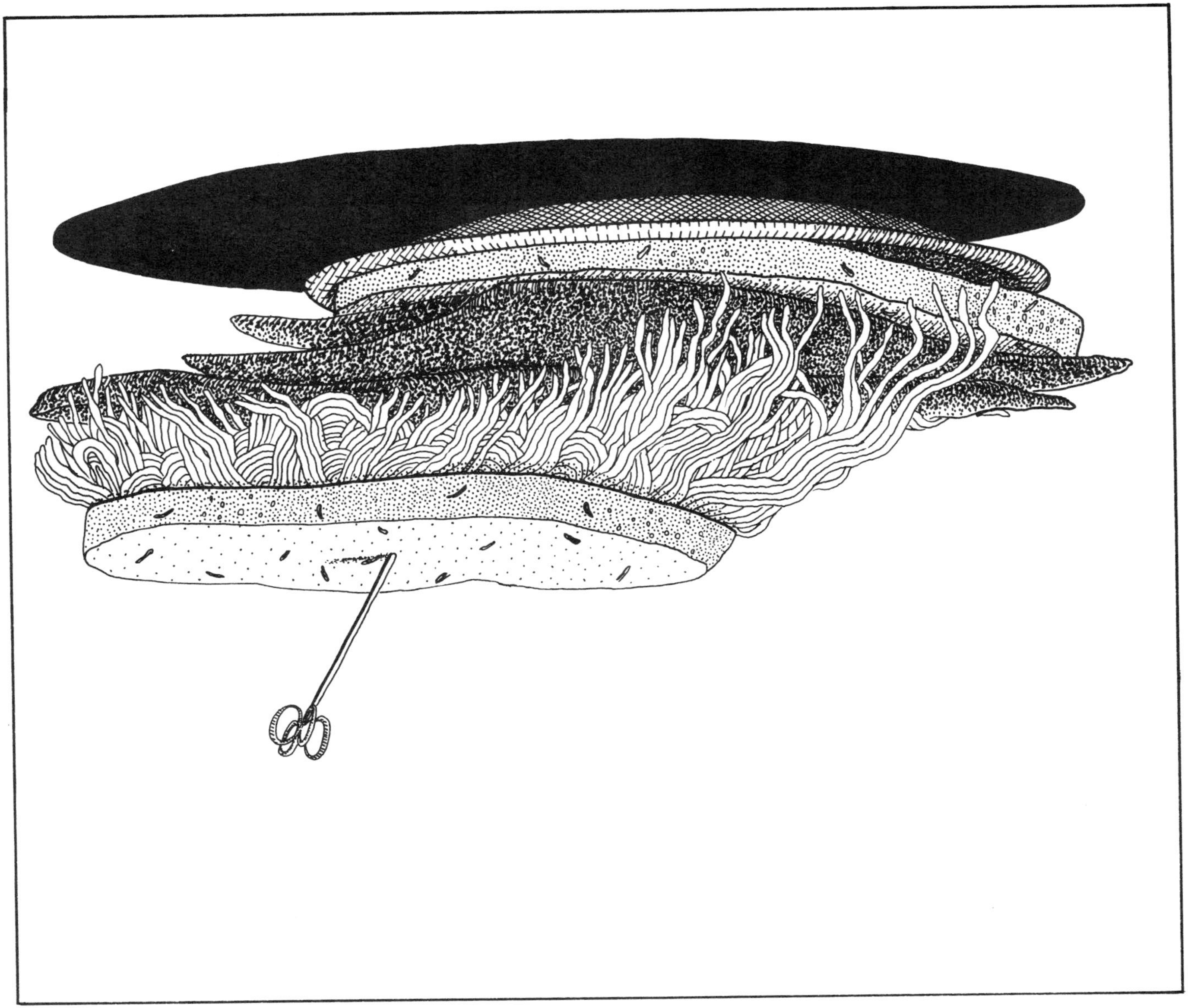

chubbychecker

chuckberry

victormature

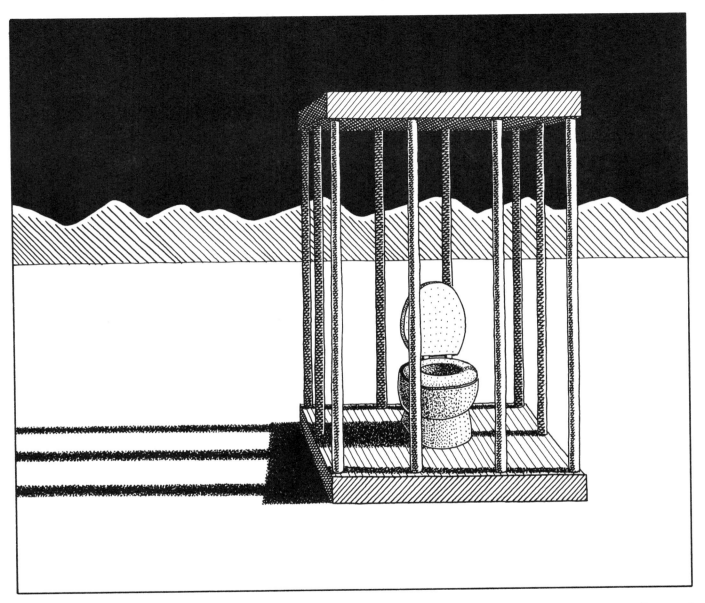

johncage

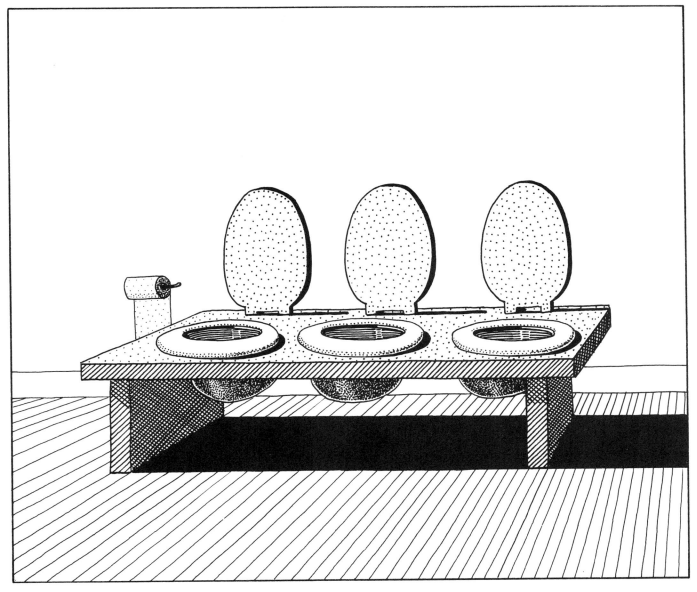

johnnybench

mozart

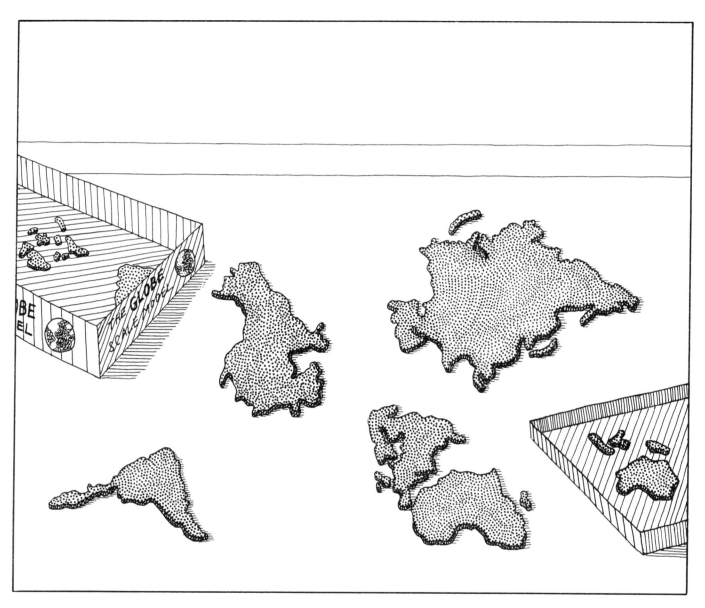

earthakitt

tabhunter.

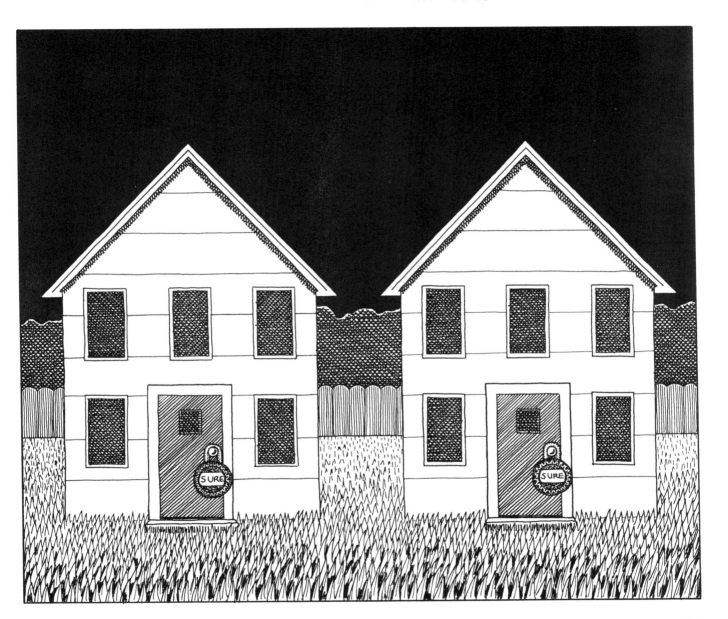

dyancannon

only $10⁰⁰

VIBRATORS

VIBRATORS

griffinbell

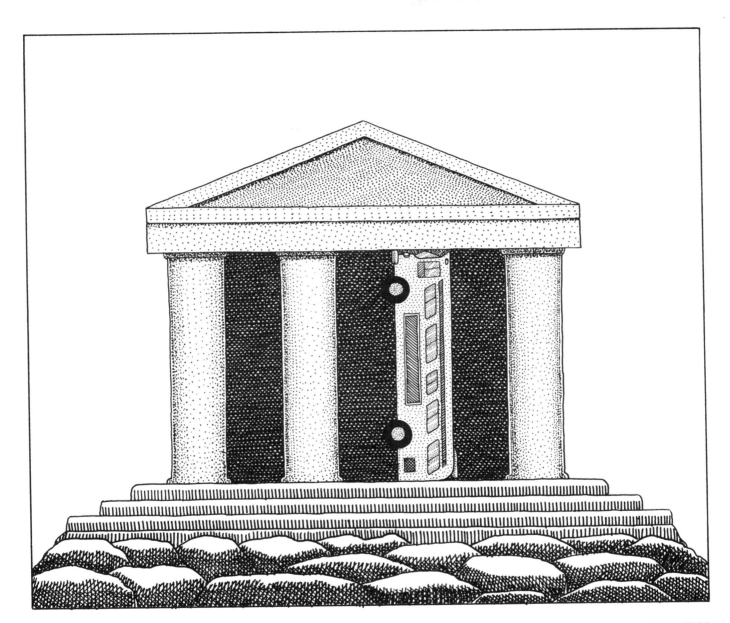

columbus

fattyarbuckle